Red Cross Dog

Red Cross Dog

POEMS

Patricia Zontelli

Headwaters 1
2000

John Ashbery, "Loving Mad Tom," published in *Houseboat Days* (New York: Penguin, 1997), copyright John Ashbery, quoted with permission; Yvonne Cartouch, "I Come to You with the Vertigoes of the Source," published in *A Book of Women Poets from Antiquity to Now: Selections from the World Over*, rev. ed., ed. Aliki Barnstone and Willis Barnstone (New York: Schocken Books, 1992). Every effort has been made to trace the appropriate copyright holders of quoted material; the publisher apologizes and asks to be notified of any inadvertent omissions.

New Rivers Press is a nonprofit literary press dedicated to publishing emerging writers.

The publication of *Red Cross Dog* has been made possible by a generous grant provided by the Minnesota State Arts Board, through an appropriation by the Minnesota State Legislature. In addition, this activity is supported by a grant from the National Endowment for the Arts.

Additional support has been provided by the General Mills Foundation, the McKnight Foundation, the Star Tribune Foundation, and the contributing members of New Rivers Press.

NATIONAL
ENDOWMENT
FOR THE
ARTS

MINNESOTA
STATE ARTS BOARD

New Rivers Press
420 North Fifth Street Suite 1180
Minneapolis, MN 55401

www.newriverspress.org

For Charles

And in an orgy of minutes the waiting
Seeks to continue, to begin again,
Amid bugs, the barking of dogs, all the
Maddening irregularities of trees, and night falls anyway.

JOHN ASHBERY, *HOUSEBOAT DAYS*
("LOVING MAD TOM")

CONTENTS

I. Red Cross Dog

II. Backward/Forward

III. Morton Salt® Girl

I

Red Cross Dog

"They say that he passed by as a dog was being beaten, and pitying it, spoke these words: 'Stop, and do not beat it; the animal has the soul of a friend; I know this, for I heard it speak.'"

PYTHAGORAS, AS RECORDED
BY XENOPHANES

"You only *think* you're barking at nothing. We're *all* barking at *something*."

LEO CULLUM, CARTOON, *NEW YORKER*
(PSYCHIATRIST TO DOG STRETCHED
OUT ON HIS COUCH)

ALL I CAN DO

I am the reason someone gets up
in the morning; I am the Red Cross Dog

and I notice how the country heaves
with unrest, how right before snow falls

the air smells like lightning (it's then
I dream of cut grass and flying stars) —

all the while, there is that deep rumble
in the distance, and even though I am minding

my own business and even though there is someone
telling me "Red Cross Dog, I know you'll help me

find my way back home," I cannot forget
that my country is falling and I cannot pick

it up. I cannot do this.

SIGNALS

I have heard that the dead
speak to the living; they may be
gone for years when out of nowhere
a voice says, "Bob, this is your mother
talking: stop it." And he'll put down
the big wrench he had threatened
the little guy's head with and go home
to bed. We think the dead
have forgotten us and then they send
signals that they have not forgotten, that
they are right there beside us or in the corner
of the kitchen by my blue water bowl,
my full food bowl, something behind me
wagging like crazy which could be my tail
but is not; I believe it is the tail of my
dead Dad; he is saying in his own way,
"You know, you really deserve this good life."

RED CROSS DOG

I am the dog
inside of all of you.
I am the bared teeth,
the drool, the leap

into light. I am
the nicest creature you've met;
I am the worst.
   I am

your nightmare: yourself
as beast. Entirely
dependent on whims,
    moods,

the need for *fetch*
and *bring*. Your leash
to my neck passed hand to
hand through centuries.

RED CROSS DOG
AT PRAYER

Here's to anorexics bending
to lace their shoes.
Here's to the dead passing
back their news.
Here's to convicts stumbling
in their stripes.
Here's to academics choking
on their pipes.
Here's to the exile waiting
for a letter.
Here's to the terminal trying
to get better.
Here's to lovers, angry and sad.
Here's to other dogs like me: bad,
mad, vulnerable.

MY COMRADE, THE BAD DOG

The kind of dog who'd plunge
his teeth deep into the bowl of chow,
never stop to breathe until it
was empty. Beaten as a pup, now
he beats back. He growls at
any living thing; he growls at oaks.
Cantankerous, contemptible, his howls
contaminate. In daylight, he claws
the walls of his house. At dusk,
he puts on his blackest sunglasses, his
leather collar with the metal spikes,
slinks out to bury his fears, his
unconquerable fears, under
the blue-black smear of night.

RED CROSS DOG
CONTEMPLATES
THE UNIVERSE

After supper dishes—water bowl,
food bowl—a quick swab
around the microwave
—he begins where he left off:
reading his way into what's
left of the evening.
    All week he's returned
to one book, *The Relative Sizes
of Planets,* illustrated
in proportional scale from the sun.
He loves the details of the planets,
their major moons. His favorite,
Pluto, is so far from the sun it takes
over 200 years to complete one orbit;
the Red Cross Dog is lost in the height
of the stars, long shining shafts
of light that call through the night—
bigger than life, frictionless molecules
powerful as desire. Out there.

DOG DAYS

It's nearing 105°, sun a sultry eye.
I pant on my porch floor, my tongue
rolled out before me. At night,
I howl, freeing my soul. All
around the town, howls join mine.
A man calls to me in his sleep—
"Red Cross Dog, the moon has fallen
in the scum-covered lake!" In the alley
a young woman rakes the inside of her arm
with a safety pin. She spends her days
rescuing paper bags from garbage bins,
folding them, tying them carefully
with twine. I lift my head.
Everything will be all right, I say.
All that you'll ever need is here
in this soiled, boiling minute.
Outside, more howls start up. These August
days and nights lope like wolves into autumn.

GUARD DOG

I shall guard your gold,
your false teeth, your fur
slippers, your morning
breath, your cake.
If a burglar comes, I'll bark
myself inside out. I'll
never tire. Count on me
to: fetch, carry, jump, heel,
lick your hand, roll over,
stare at you across distances
like a lover. When I die,
I will be the two eyes
that sit in the darkness
of your wardrobe. When I die,
as moonlight shines upon my
white bones, I will still
guard you as a ghost would,
lurking in the shadow world,
in the blank vagaries of your
memory of me, my eternal furry
presence; my barely perceptible,
about-to-break-loose growl
freeing you
from everything you fear.

Frisbee

Over and over, I catch
what I can, and
having caught it,
drop it: wet,

glistening, at the feet
of the woman on the lawn
who doesn't want to go inside
her house just yet, who

doesn't want to go inside
her house at all, who needs
me, the Red Cross Dog,
to give her a reason

for one more minute to
herself, one more minute
to search the late-day sky
for something to come

sailing down to her, like
good luck for a change:
a piece of the moon.

WILD DOG

runs in me still. There are times
as I lope through the battered dark

of a night heavy with crying
and one white round moon,

I am wolf. My yellow eyes burn
fluorescent in cars' headlights, muscles

of my grin stiffen, my lips
draw back in a snarl. I pad forward

silently, at a faster clip
—then, I'm bounding, saliva flying.

Please.
Stay out of my way when I'm like this.

I'll go for your face. Your little one's
soft, fat leg.

In the Attic, under the Skylight

In the attic, the Red Cross Dog works
his way through a stack of curling photos;
he is looking for his past.
It is one hour until dawn. He peers
into the photographs, tries
to remember the evening: the young dog
there beside him in the long dress,
flowers at her wrist. He can't
recall her name or what she looked
like in color. When he glances up
at the moon, it does not come
rushing back to him, the way moonlight
played over her fur or anything like that.
He only knows that, though she loved
to dance and he couldn't, she sat
at the table smiling her big smile,
swaying her narrow shoulders to music
of a band that didn't stop.
He flips through the photo album, half
of it blank where something should have been.
The Red Cross Dog is tired now; he is slipping
like a house over sand, like a photograph
so past its time that even to hold it
to moonlight would fade it forever.

MIDNIGHT

The Red Cross Dog meanders over to the bus
station, sees the occupants trying to sleep
on the plastic bucket chairs designed
for sitting sharply upward, sees the mother
with the four kids sleeping against her
in the corner on the floor,
the only mountain they need. He
snuffles the pockmarked linoleum
for Cheezie discards to lick, finds
the bandaged foot of a woman in homemade
sandals, her brown grocery bag of belongings
on her lap. She holds out to him a half-eaten
bologna on white. He licks every last crumb,
even the ones fallen on her foot, between
her moist, delicious toes. He slumps there,
curled around her foot. All night,
her hand caresses his back as if his fur
was the long warm grass of the hillside behind
her childhood house. As if he were the hill itself.

MORNING

The bus station smells like a bag of burgers
has been stuffed behind a seat, left there for weeks.
Red Cross Dog decides he needs to get up, stretch,
maybe head for home. Light sneaks through
the bleary front doors that let in morning street
sounds and more people coming in from the fringe
to wash, wrap fingers around coffee cups, warm
themselves over the register. A few even buy tickets,
shaking out the dark cloth of their lives to
take off to a particular somewhere, anywhere.
The Dog thinks, *I'd* love to travel, hit the trails,
sniff out some new shadows. He knows there is much
to do here, much expected. It's worth my while,
he decides, to stay here among the travelers
and the hard luck, for all those souls who seem
to need to sink their hands into my thick fur,
acknowledge me in their own language.

MISSION

Red Cross Dog's on a mission, so secret
even he doesn't know where, why, when. But

he's up for it. So late one night he wraps
two blackened bratwursts in wax paper, straps

his canvas bag around his middle, and disappears.
He doesn't return the next day or the next.

The third day, he's back, worn out and salivating,
fur a mess. There is a whisper of exotic scent

in the air and on his face a smile like that of one
who's done something so improbable even he

didn't know he could do it. He'd do it again.

RED CROSS DOG
AT HOME

It's after midnight.
All lights are off. It's then

I relax. Upstairs, my master snores,
dreaming of more.

Downstairs, I sprawl, lick
my balls, sniff the cheese drift

of his dropped socks. The room
is quiet, TV turned off: no

blue light arcing air,
no rattle and bang, no reports

from the inner city nip,
nip, nipping at my heart.

RED CROSS DOG
AT HOME — II

Outside, night in this city
is never still or silent.

Ambulances and trucks weave
through evening shadows like animals,

the air reeking of wounds.
The fires of the homeless flare and

smudge into mist that rises

past windows of rooms
where the TV stays on all night

unseen, unheard — blue balm
for all those frightened

of the looming, the careening.

Spooks

There is the Ku Klux Klan.
There are the ones on planes
with odd missions; there are the ones
in the woods of northern Michigan.
And all the others: relatives
who cannot forgive;
apple-polishers who'll
say anything; dog-haters
who'll say nothing until
they get you alone in a room.

Day before Winter

My four legs are wearing the day out:
what a day! In the park, the trees
send down their avalanche of leaves—
some of them escaping, like birds, into air.
The river passes, cutting
its diamonds loose, calling to me,
imploring me, *just keep on walking—*
what needs to be found will be found.
I sniff, lick one rich garbage bag
after another. The sky is blue, resolute.
Under it, nothing is ambiguous—
the red, blue, green cars passing and re-
passing; the faces of the joggers bob
and glow, the leaves endlessly turning color
and whirling away, as in a film where a dog
is running down a road barking, warning
that something is happening so fast
that however ordinary and safe and gorgeous
this moment is, it is ending.

So Much Expected

I am the one slated to save
the runaway child, to lead

back home the lost, the drugged,
the disappeared—and by

extraordinary constancy and good-
deed example, to be the best

that lives in all of us—like
Rin Tin Tin flickering through

the grainy black/white forest
to find the lost child, or like Lassie,

plunging into the burning house.
Goodie Two Shoes. But with

four legs, fur, one brief life.

Loss

Digging up the bones. Reburying them.
Digging up the bones to see if they're still there.
Reburying them. Digging up the bones
to lick them one more time—licking them white
one more time under the white moon.
Burying them. Digging them up, just
to smell them, sniff any trace
of life there. Reburying them. Digging them up
to relieve the itch of my desire to see them,
to inhale their fading odor of blood, to
polish their hollows with my tongue,
turning them into something else, something
only I will recognize now. Burying them
in a place where even I can't find them.

II

Backward/Forward

A Deer Hangs in a Neighbor's Yard

Slowly under an oak, the buck
swings from the rope
tied to his antlers

stiff legs brush tall grass
as if to smooth the restless
gestures of the field, moving

as in a dream of movement:
air rushes between his antlers
as he runs, building speed,
hooves cut dry leaves to powder

the forest stutters beneath him.
He begins his long free fall
into a lake so cold
a mirror of ice forms

over his eyes.
He stares at all—

haze blurred into wet blooms
so untamed, lush

that even as his legs drift and slur
into their tired parody of waltz

he cannot stop staring—as on

that day of another autumn when I stared
at the rope twisting over the head of my
friend, blur of police light
twirling over his yellow T-shirt, his feet

barely hurting the garage floor,
feet just missing the dance.

WIND

       shakes
the house, yowls
like a lost ancestor, drags
snow down off our roofs,
makes it look like it's snowing
even when it's not.
At the edge of fields
drifts an old voice,
carried by wind.
It tells you:
learn the language
of whatever's out there.
Tracks are covered over,
swept by wind. *Who*
was here?
You shout into the wind;
it swallows your sound,
it dissolves light—it
warns you we are all elements,
that something ancient, glacial,
moves just outside our walls.

Log Cabin

The logs roll even when
chinked and mortared: six o'clock
mornings, the whole room tilts

with light. Outdoors
in frantic wind, the pines wave,
"See me, See me"

crossing and recrossing
their long shaggy arms
in front of themselves

like the first on the scene
of an accident, flagging down cars.

Cloud

Under the tall oak, the small house
cannot sleep. Downstairs, on walls
of narrow rooms, cars' headlights
take careless aim. Upstairs, windows
tell passersby someone inside breathes.
A man in flannel pajamas wraps
his arms around himself as he stares
out at the cold trees. Around him,
the stiffness of objects. A wooden
chair with straight back. A pair
of scissors open on the bedside table.
One glass. The cold inside him tightens;
a woman's voice whispers to him
in a half-dream. He sees her hurt face,
her longing, sees the two
of them traveling together in the dark
above the trees, so close together
they merge, become one shape—
quiet and decent as a cloud
passing over a house.

Black and White

Squatting on the flat rock
in the garden, I shuck sweet corn
before supper,
pulling its fine movie-starlet hair

down into a brown grocery bag.
A swish behind. I turn,
see three skunks: a mother
trailed by two young ones

plumed tails straight up—in rhythmic
unison they flaunt the daylight,
ambling regal as drag queens
in their fringe and dark-light stripes

padding their way toward high weeds
behind the wood shed. I creep
sideways to the house to call the children;
when we come out, they are gone.

Later that week, my car thumping
with my teenage daughter's rock 'n' roll,
I swerve to avoid a black-white carcass,
its ratty tags of pink meat; its scent

trapped in my wheels. For weeks after,
any heat brings three shapes
blundering into view
—untethered, stunning as movie stars.

ANNA CHRISTINA JOHNSON
PLAYS THE SAW

For her five children, she sewed
clothes, baked meat and potatoes
and worked two jobs, two shifts.

For her Presbyterian church,
she vibrated with such ardent
hymns of thanksgiving

the cherries on her felt hat shook, her shy
divorced son, Howard, shrinking down
into the pockets of his Sunday suit. Anna's

entire backyard sprouted garden, not a weed
dared—everything edible glassed into quarts
for Howard, diabetic until at forty-three

he died of it—and of that other,
an unmended heart. For herself,
Anna played the saw

in the cellar, amidst the coal smell, coal
furnace, jars of pickles, pears, piccalilli,
chow-chow, melon rind and rhubarb;

under a bare lightbulb my grandmother Anna
played the saw, wiggling the tip
of it "just so" to make the eerie

unpredictable Norwegian melody flitter
into air, with such
stubbornness in her blue eyes that

the house danced, the garden swayed,
the glass wind chime
on her front porch shivered

its careful, delicate applause.

POTATOES

To keep them from freezing, from turning
black in the night
he hugged the sack to his own heat
inside the one-room sod house
staking his one-year one-day homestead claim.
How snow filled that North Dakota year.
Forgetting the potatoes, doped with sleep,
he rolled over onto them and half awoke
with the dream of falling down a hill onto
rocks. There beside a stilled stream
a woman slices potatoes into a pan
of sizzling fat, her face intent
over the campfire, calm as Anna Christina
who would be my grandmother.
And he awoke, releasing the sack, alert
to the silence of his house, the emptiness
of his arms. There, beyond his one small window
facing east, dawnlight began its slow slide
over the frozen land to touch and touch again
his roof, his window of ice.

STARS

have fallen on the frozen window.
I can barely see out, night's
black shards growing stories.
Tonight, I understand cold,
what it is for—
the simple complexity of moisture
collected on glass, the breath
of all who've passed through
this house:
shifting dream slate, stars
falling, stars connecting.

F LOOD

The river rose.
There came a refrigerator

floating on its back.
Still, the river rose,

four snakes swimming
on the crest.

Everything gone
or wrecked:

even when the water left,
it was as if

it was still here,
licking, nudging everything

inside, outside my house.
The flood marks its territory

like a dog in my dreams. I know
it will make its way back.

"NUDE MODEL WIFE LEAVES ARTIST"

She hears the will of mallards overhead pull
straight toward blue light, pink islands of heat.

Then he appears, takes up his brush: *slap, slap*
against canvas. There is music, something jokey,

on the old phonograph. He commands:
Dance. They polka to the other side

of the studio. She trips. He swears to turn her
into a still life.

She pleads.
He paints.

The moon closes over her eyes. In the dark night
a mallard calls her name. She listens. Again

and again, it calls. Her hair spreads behind her
like a fan, first one bare foot leaves the floor,

then the other.

FRIDA

KAHLO comes back, disguised
as a woman selling cosmetics
at the drugstore. We are stunned
by her eyebrows, her authority,
the monkey on one shoulder. She pleads,
begs us to decorate ourselves
with viridian green hope
tinged with red. Put
some barbed wire there beside
the nostril. Pinch the cheeks
cerise, coral. Penetrate
the back of the head with sharp
combs shaped like parrots. If
there is a hole in your heart,
she'll say, wrap it in silk. But
leave the slit on your neck open.

✦

FRIDA is meeting me after work
at the crossing of bones and veins.
I am smoking. She carries her womb
in a bucket. Today, she is dressed as a man,
all her brown hair shorn, fallen in wisps
around her like whispers or the frail
brown fingers of the dead. The dead
are alive to Frida. The dead are meat
and potatoes. "Let us hang their bones

above our beds," she says, accepting
a cigarette. "They remind us."

✦

MY MOTHER is coming to meet me
on the steps of the green laundromat.
She's carrying her load of old laundry,
her bucket of jazz and swing sung
at the kitchen table. I'm underneath,
pinching clothespins on my fingers.
She sings to the portable radio, plastic
and yellow. She is singing for my father
who won't come home. She is singing
for the twin-tub Maytag—which swills
the gray water twice; she wrings
and hangs and sings. And we wait.

✦

FRIDA is doing her laundry in her head:
her magenta rebozo twirls with her red
rebozo; her alizarin crimson dress holds hands
with her green nightgown; her exquisite man's

tweed suit wrinkles and unwrinkles; the heads
of Trotsky and Lenin spin; Diego Rivera bends
to kiss the lips of her sister, Christina, his hands
wave good-bye to Frida in the water; her bucket lands

on the floor, soapy water streams over the cold
tiles under her feet, rushes under her iron bed.

♦

"AT NIGHT, the dark part
of the jungle
is my iron bed,
its canopy
of vein, leaf, root.
It is late.
It is quiet.
There are no children
for miles.
I close my eyes,
hear the faint hoofbeats
of my deer, Graniza,
in the undergrowth.
My two cockatoos
shake the starched
petticoats of their
wings, my monkey
swings on vines
toward me,
its long, black arms
reach for me. My old parrot
sits in the moonlight;
though her bill
is cracked,
her feathers are fine;
she is colorful, resplendent
as a clown. 'Stay awake,'
she instructs. 'Stay awake.'"

✦

FIRST, she paints herself.
Then, she paints herself.
She holds hands with herself
as she looks at herself in the mirror.
She likes staring at her possibilities;
all that hair, those wide eyes,
the mustache, the eyebrows
that link above her eyes.
Behind her, the world slips
and shoves; her own life hits
her in the throat. The hand
that holds the brush is steady.

✦

"RED: how much I have been through
to be here for this one morning.
Be careful with this color. Someone
is cutting off my leg. My God, where is
my child? Is this a dream or vision?
My body paints a picture of blood.
My iron bed, my canvas. Where is
my child? Let me catch the light,
just so. I can step on nails now,
they will not hurt me. Mornings like this,
I study my surroundings, forget them.
I am seeking blue all the time.
Yellow. The inconstant, reluctant green.
Where is my child? How wide can I open?"

Inside a Painting
by Magritte

Again, it rains.
Listen to the emptiness.
Like something being tried
over and over. Gulls
rise at the edge.
I spill the tea.
Water gulps onto shore.
The window opens:
the few palm trees suddenly
in their right places.
The black rose on the table
has turned red.
From my chair by my window
my eyes write
in the sand.
My words would not
surprise *you*, Magritte.
Before anyone even notices,
the light goes from gray
to brilliant green.

MOON PASSING

Its round white face
bobs up—
                    its fish eye

stares intently through
my slatted bedroom blinds,
sending wavering stripes

of light to skim across floors,
over the herringbone tufts
of the throw rug, over things

I own, sprawled, spilled
around me—to focus, shivering,
on the squared vanity mirror,

the angle of my arm
raising the tortoise comb.
Before the moment

all is caught
and measured, the light
lifts:

phosphorescent scales flash
across black; the night
is bent on rinsing

each tired day's end until
what's up there above
feels clean enough

for us to risk stepping off
the contours of this day
into morning's new space

where, even now,
light races to touch.

Backward / Forward

Undressed, lolling between her sheets
of drenching April rain,
how skillfully she conjures up
the sound of moths winking, their image
of greedy gourmet dreams:
thick wool sweaters lying bunched
in the attic box. Later

under the stare of May sun
she stretches on her hammock
of swinging lawn shadows,
gathers herself up, out, and—lifting
her green ruffled skirts above her head—howls
uproariously, shaking her long
maidenhair ferns down from the suspended
twists and turns of light. At night

she takes out her sleeping bag
of wood ticks, groping bird eggs,
Creeping Charlie—it is then, under dark,
she hatches her scented plots
and gossips to herself for hours on end, knowing
that though we're not all she'd wish us to be
at least there is something hopeful:
the way we brag about
taking the longest route home,
the one that passes Gieske's Bay
where "lilacs are at their best now"

the way that, even as we reward the children
one cent for every swatted fly,
we take a moment to explain
the complexities of the species' eyes—
how they see in ways we cannot
hope to—backward/forward
in the same minute blackspeck of time.

WINDOWFUL OF BIRDS

It's like an airport
        out there—
        think of how they come
only to leave

settling like tourists
        for brief bites,
        got-to-run looks
in their black, clicking eyes

how clearly they resemble
        clockwork toys
        in their animated
kicking, hopping

—flicking seeds off feeders,
        pecking out codes
        scrabbling onto
snow's crust their

intricate, particular signals.
        Think of them—handfuls of
        bone, feather, skin
tossed in the harsh open bowl

of wind. Somehow, they've
found the trick of it,
riding winter storms
—to land,

right side up,
small shadows taxiing in
from across the world
for our crumbs,

our handful of seeds.

Ouija

                    The unpredictable happens
to ordinary beings like me; there is always that

element of chance. I know simple geometric shape
is inhuman; I know flocks of grape-

dark birds define the air, that the fog
is loaded down with mistrust—dialogue

constantly going forward/backward—words roam
around the room. I believe in the ghosts

that know they are dead, the ghosts
that know they are posthumously

needed. Treading water, I think I should
swim. Thrashing, kicking, I wish I could

return to that point where all I had to think
was *float* and I floated, dark birds in the blink

of air overhead—carefree but
stunning as letters of an unknown, fugitive alphabet.

Naming the Water

What are the words for layers of color
the lake divides itself into, layers
growing cooler as we move toward the bottom?
Thrusting upward, gasping for air,
we rock with the waves, synchronously
mocking their movement; what
is the name for this dance?
What is the name for pockets of warmth
found even in deepest water?
And what do you call the pull
of water, the attraction we have
to lakes, rivers, seas? Our bodies
move like mermaids toward
bodies of water, however far,
however calm or wild.

To the Lake

Powerful enough to pull me into you
even at dawn; strong enough for me to walk
your frozen back, strange enough to
sing to me with your loon calls and fish slaps;
large enough to keep me from swimming
across, storm clouds laughing.
The summer I was thirteen and knew with sudden
clarity I was crazy, I sat up in bed
in the middle of night listening for messages
and heard you: I entered
in the warm dark, your water
calming me, your whispering mouth
in my ear:
You are real. This lake is real. This
shivering is real.

ALL THE
RAISED ARMS

We are afraid of the lake,
the sun that stuns the sky,
the orchid quiet
of the water. *It has*
taken a life today.
The water circles.
Rings around rings, over
spirals we cannot see
but know are there, that
are like ropes that pull
the ones we love
down to its body,
—the body that restrains
the arms of those
who struggle to rise
and wave to us as one,
two and three down—
they drown,

         they drown.

STILL CENTER

Alone. It's
as if no one else exists anywhere.
And so much noise. The *lip, lip* of
water pressing boat walls; the creak
of oarlock; flick of dragonflies;

lake flat as a table I lay my thoughts
upon, like so many papers: shuffled,
arranged. For the first time
in a long while, no clutter. My mind trim,

in order. I place my hand flat upon water,
feel the stones' weight underneath my boat; feel
fern algae arc and wave; feel the fish, whatever
it is they have for hearts, pumping, ticking.

The shoreline pulls back further.

SMALL LAKE UP NORTH

It is true, I love this small
round lake—to look at it

is to enter past and future; the lake
was here, the lake will always be here.

I sit, watch it divide itself
into colors. In daylight

it carries my boat, my body. On
calm nights, it holds the moon's reflection

for so long I scarcely notice when,
with the smallest breeze, its silver tray spills—

the lake becomes a plateful of stars.
Tomorrow, when I enter my boat

and row to the center,
I will listen for the loon's call, its

delirium, its undertow of longing—
and know that the lake, hushed under its

surface of nerves, also listens.

Night Swim

I go for a night swim
in the dusk hour: so this
is what it's like to live.
I dip, spurt like a dolphin,
heart beating madly
as a muskrat paddles out—
taking the night air
in his city, twirling his mustache.

        Evening brings
the slow dark, the panting but
hushed self, elderberry bush
mere shadow. Dog Star,
up there as usual, eyes
us below like so many bones,
protectively. All treachery eased.

Here I am, not in water but,
at this late warm hour, still sitting
on the grassy bank. Maybe it's true,
I can grow old gracefully. Tonight,
I look into the dark with no regret.
I'm happy here, in this body,
these bones, uncomplicated
by glare, heat of sunlight.

FIREFLIES

The present: a place
so thick I use all
my muscle to push up, out of,

back to the world at dusk:
    a cloud of fireflies

each burning fleck accepting me
as if I too could fly
blink light   drift

with them through a life
of warm summer evenings

—the sighting of a swarm of us
a gift to all who watch.
        Now

I want to fall through the years,
touch the innocent heart
of myself:

    head filling with stars
my whole life before me
        out there

    above the grass.

FIRST WARM DAY

A month from now,
we'll open sleep
with windows. First
warm day, birds,
frantic with release,
will escape trees
perched on the edge
—the flat lake a mirror
we can forget
ourselves in, that holds
what it sees
only as long
as it takes to receive,
give back light,
color: a generosity
of green.

You Understood

For J. L. and R. L.

You understood the wonder of the trees
were those many greens of early spring
when all was before us, when hope shimmered
like light hitting that glass of orange juice
as you raised it in a toast

to getting through one more night without the morphine.
You understood that love is a mental exercise
twelve steps up from the physical, though that was
important enough to regret. Then,

one more long, slow walk in the woods.
The trees didn't let us down: a maple limb
snapped, a lilac broke gently into flower.
Take me, it said. *I'm yours for the taking.*
Instead, you took my hand.

GOING TO WORK

Today, spring arrived as if it had come
a long way, loaded down with hints, remnants,
scents of such complexity its actual presence
here seems a miracle: I will regard it
as such. I'm driving to work and all I see
are green arms waving at me—ecstatically—
from both sides of the street, grass
acting like it's just been discovered—
and in the parking lot where I generally don't
linger, I linger today because a hundred
crocuses are just this minute opening their mouths
at the edge. I enter the metal cave
of the loading dock conducting an orchestra.

III

Morton Salt® Girl

MORTON SALT® GIRL

I walk corridors of rain
—the one I fear sleeps
as I slip by in the downpour
with my cylinder of salt, my
umbrella; crackling yellow
unzips heavy clouds;

I hurry past thin walls,
stone fences, past houses
crumbling into the mist.
There are times I
walk so far so fast

my life widens; I enter
familiar rooms that turn
in lamplight, starlight:

my stepfather at the window
with blood on his hands,
grandmother correcting her hat
in the mirror

the urgent dogbark of my plan:
go forward, carry the box, keep
silent, pass through curtains

of water. Salt falls, dissolves;
I walk through rain into my life.

Yellow

She is exhausted, but will not
go to the houses with yellow light
pouring over their sills

She's exhausted, but will not
stop at the house with daisy-
papered walls, fireplace gold
playing over the tablecloth,
steam rising from the roast turkey,
goblets of warmed wine.

She's exhausted, but will not
enter the room with the light
in the corner, the narrow bed,
the man who locks
the door, takes her umbrella,
presses her face against
the wood headboard,
opens something inside her.

BLACK

The moon was falling through the sky
darkness stepped out of its house
as her stepfather
stepped out of his mind:
all day he'd been waiting.

DARK

She cannot say
where her stepfather is now:
hands like worms crawling, breath
like a dog that eats its own shit.
Now he could be anywhere
squeezed into blackest shadow,
dirt under a thumbnail.

LAKE

Her body, a shadow,
trails. His voice
traces the way fingers
float through hair, sun
under water. Those days
she was lost in patterns,
rain on the lake,
swirls. Last day,
he had her on the cabin
floor. Don't tell
your mother; don't tell
anyone. As he drove
them home, she watched
numb, as two deer came through
their car lights, amazed at
how easily they arrived,
departed.

MIRROR

Silence holds its breath
in the midst of a motionless wind
and the riotings of mirrors

YVONNE CAROUTCH

She had the feeling
she never quite
made sense—
in her own house,
she knew she must
be silent; no one
understood what she
could not explain.
Sifting through rooms,
past knick knacks,
past TV's snow,
it occurred
to her what she must do—
but she could not.
Mouth pressed
under glass, words
held under until all
breath went out
of them. And the girl
in the mirror
looked right through her.

STINK

He had told her that she smelled.
Because of what

she had let him do.
It was not his fault they'd

done it; it was because
of her little-nothing shorts

the ones with red lips on them.
She saved her babysitting money

for eau de cologne—extralarge bottles
of Xanadu at Discount Drugs; she diluted

Hi-lex to wash her private parts, scrubbing
until she stung. It didn't help.

Riding the school bus home, she heard
the kids. "Don't sit near her. She smells."

DREAMCARD

He flings himself down upon the carpet
with a postcard in his hand—
disappears inside it,

warm waterfalls umbrella over his naked body,
snails beneath his feet crack,
ooze. It is dusk. The flamboyant parrots

flap off. He backs out of his jungle
peeling a nearly green banana. Grandmother
watching behind her palm, closes her eyes

as he roars, arms flaying, grabbing me by the hair
as he swings into the rectangle of night
where the moon pours its soured milk

onto trees. Blue snakes tangle, untangle
in the clearing where he makes me do it.
And not one star sees.

S N O W

There was snow. She is six.
The lake hard as a window.
Her skateblades cut side to side.
A woman, her mother—
pulling her mittened hands—has just
heard something that hurt her.
Her eyes shine—the ice, their skateblades
shine. A man with no coat waves
from the snowy boundaries
of the lake, fists in air, white clouds
of words rising furiously above him.
The girl and her mother skate out
to the center of the lake
where there are no edges, no noise except
the gash, gash of their sharp blades.

Circles

Lying in bed, a bed of hay
in a barn off Highway Seven,
one arm cocked behind
her head, her other encircling
the salt cylinder, she thinks
of her future, what she wants
the world to say of her:
She had to lie to tell the truth
or *She never cried no matter what*

    Or

She was not polite. She
laughed aloud at that one,
smearing drops from the damp hay
onto her face, beginning the ritual
that keeps him away, the slow
exact movement of hand on wrist;
take a little salt. Rub in circles.
Rub hard, harder into the cuts.

Storm

Crouched at midnight
under a state park
picnic table, the girl
thinks of things
she cannot see but knows
are there: insects, bats,
the wild limbs of the dead.
And then she settles. Awakened
by thunder, she watches
trees move, dark green
hunched animals
lurching in wind—
lightning flinging its flares
—park lawn on fire then
not on fire—
its edges licked
by light, the hedges caught
snapshot still: green
leaves turned white.
Beneath the hedges, its
pink eyes flickering,
a rabbit's head lies
grinning in the grass.

SHIFT

Salt does not stand still;
it shifts. The girl
does not stay long anywhere.
She's happiest on wheels. She thanks
the woman in the plastic rainhat
who drops her at the curb. "My aunt
lives just there—in that blue
place . . ." Salt, putting on its best
disappearing act when it's wet,
blends. She's careful not to
litter, leave prints, any scrap
of name; what chalk trace there is,
he'll find. She walks this new main street,
looks hard into face after face, relieved.
In thin drizzle she imagines snow
or salt falling; a home movie, grainy,
abstract but real, real
but abstract: her family gathered—
mother, grandmother, stepfather and her—
smiling, hugging each other, the scene
hysterically speeded up to an almost
bearable blur.

SECRET

The night speaks to her
as if it's been waiting.
She cannot sleep.
Night grows impatient, its dark
hive hums round her head.
*Speak   Say   Tell
what he's done.* Night
presses its damp face close
to hers. *Speak* says the night.
She cannot unfold her tongue.
Say says the shadow. Words
swim in her mouth, bob
to the surface. *Tell*
says the bee circling her head
as her voice flies out of her mouth.

S KATE

In her dream she holds big kitchen matches over the cold
of it, the girl is careful but constantly

misses the shoreline; it is always lost. Her dog jumps
at the edge, reeds

rasp, the little dog barks, wind bites. She wants to flee
him, his voice

white, mouth open. There is a wide ring under ice, her step-
father under ice where blood pools

black under deep, the pickerel swish and pike sink
and swim, her quick blades slash, then

she makes him vanish, figure 8's hazy behind her, the dog
waving his brown paw, abrupt

booms under ice, anxious circles erased, a time loop, circles
under her eyes smoothed, all movement

erased; at last she spins outlines, skims numerals, finally
words: *help. This is what he has*

done to me. Then and then her pink ear placed briefly down
against cold thin glass, a large weight

rising, she lights match after match, light presses against
the darkness surrounding her:

smoking matches, the smoking candles, the small dog barks
its closeness, its smoke; again and again

she tells the secret.

Ribbons

The thin ribbons of water she walks through
trickle over her body.
She's beginning to know what it's like
to give herself away.
She's beginning to know what it's like
to forgive herself for her innocence.

And there, right before her, the green grass lifts
into points, the rinsed earth solid beneath her feet.

Now

I've spilled salt—
I know I'm worth it.
Finally, I get the picture:
me in my bright yellow raincoat,
top of a hill, holding my pose,
turning whatever I choose
into salt, white statues
sprinkled by moonlight.

ACKNOWLEDGMENTS

I wish to thank the Bush Foundation for the fellowship and the Wisconsin Arts Board for the study grant that made the completion of this collection possible. I am grateful to members of my Menomonie writers' group: Robert Horan, Warren Lang, Bill O'Neill, and Anne Running. Thanks, also, to the generous instructors at the Loft Literary Center, Minneapolis; they opened the skylight to writing for me. To my Australian-English friend-poet Katherine Gallagher, I owe a special debt, for her encouragement and advice through the years.

Grateful acknowledgment is made to my New Rivers Press editors, Robert Alexander, Eric Braun, and Mary Byers, as well as to the editors of the publications in which earlier versions of the following poems appeared:

Connecticut Review, "Inside a Painting by Magritte"
Folio: A Literary Journal, "Nude Model Wife Leaves Artist"
North Coast Review, "Wind"
Northern Plains Quarterly, "Fireflies"
Piedmont Literary Review, "Log Cabin"
Spoon River Poetry Review, "Backward/Forward"
The Talking of Hands (anthology, New Rivers Press),
    "Loss" and "Signals"
There Lies a Fair Land (anthology, New Rivers Press),
    "Anna Christina Johnson Plays the Saw"
Wisconsin Academy Review, "Morton Salt Girl," "Circles,"
    "Secret"
Wisconsin Review, "The Stars"

Photo: Charles Wimmer

Patricia Zontelli received an M.F.A. from the University of Minnesota in painting and printmaking. New Rivers Press published her first poetry collection, *Edith Jacobson Begins to Fly*, as part of the Minnesota Voices Project. Zontelli has been awarded a Bush Foundation Fellowship in Literature and has won the Loft Mentor Series and Lake Superior Regional Writers Series in Poetry. *Red Cross Dog* was a finalist for the National Poetry Series and the Akron Poetry Prize. Zontelli divides her time between London, England, and Menomonie, Wisconsin. She teaches at the University of Wisconsin, Stout.